Writer's Notebook

GRADE 4

Grade **4**

Contents

MODULE 1: Personal Narrative

MODULE 2: Description

MODULE 3: Description

MODULE 4: Story

Name _____

Word Bank

As you listen to *La Mariposa* and think about your own personal narrative, jot down any interesting words and phrases. You can use this Word Bank as a resource as you draft and revise your writing.

Name _____

Personal Narrative Rubric

Use this rubric to develop and revise your personal narrative draft. For each category, ask yourself if the statement describes your narrative. As you draft and revise, set a goal to score a 4 in each category.

	Organization	Ideas & Support	Conventions
Score 4	My narrative is told in order, and the events are clearly connected.	My narrative has a clear setting, and the events are described with detail.	• My ideas are linked with words and phrases. • My writing has a variety of specific, descriptive words. • My writing has no errors in spelling, grammar, capitalization, or punctuation. There are a variety of sentence types.
Score 3	My narrative is mostly told in order, and the events are mostly connected.	My narrative has a setting, and the events are described with little detail.	• Some of my ideas are linked with words and phrases. • Some of my words are specific. • My writing has some errors in spelling, grammar, capitalization, or punctuation. There is some variety of sentence types.
Score 2	My narrative has events out of order, and/or events are missing.	My narrative has only a part of the setting, and the events have little detail.	• Ideas may be linked with words or phrases. • Few words are specific. • My writing has some errors in spelling, grammar, capitalization, or punctuation. There is little variety of sentence types.
Score 1	My narrative is out of order, and the events are confusing.	My narrative does not have a setting, and/or the events are confusing.	• Ideas may not be linked with words or phrases. • No words are specific. • My writing has many errors in spelling, grammar, capitalization, or punctuation. There is no variety of sentences. Sentences are incomplete.

Name _____

My Goals

In this module, you are going to write a personal narrative. A personal narrative tells the story of an event in your life.

Good writers set goals for their writing to help guide the writing process. Think about the parts of a narrative and what you want to accomplish. Some goals have been set already. What other goals do you have? Write them on the lines below.

☐ Introduce the setting and the conflict or problem.

☐ Describe events that happened.

☐ Include dialogue.

☐ My conflict is resolved.

☐ Use correct spelling and punctuation.

☐

☐

As you plan, draft, revise, and edit your personal narrative, turn back to these goals to make sure you are meeting them.

Topic Brainstorming: Abecedarian List

Create a list of discoveries that you might want to write a personal narrative about, using the alphabet to guide you. For each letter, write down a discovery you have made that begins with that letter. The discovery could be finding something unexpected or realizing something about yourself or another person.

A. _____   N. _____

B. _____   O. _____

C. _____   P. _____

D. _____   Q. _____

E. _____   R. _____

F. _____   S. _____

G. _____   T. _____

H. _____   U. _____

I. _____   V. _____

J. _____   W. _____

K. _____   X. _____

L. _____   Y. _____

M. _____   Z. _____

Name _____

Organizing My Personal Narrative

Complete the story map to plan the structure of your personal narrative.

Characters

Conflict	Setting

Events

Conclusion

Personal Narrative

A Grand Discovery

1   Mom and I walked up the big stone steps. I craned my neck to see the huge school building. I jumped and twirled around in my excitement to start my first day of first grade. I vividly remember that day because I made a discovery.

2   "My name is Ms. Agnes, and I am going to be your teacher," said the tall lady at the front of the class. One of the first things she did was give us big sheets of paper and big fat pencils and tell us to fill that paper with writing.

3   But I didn't know how to write. My classmates bent over their papers, so I did, too. I made straight lines, I made crooked lines, I made short lines, and I made long lines. I was determined to fill the paper.

4   When there was no more room, I waved my paper at Ms. Agnes. She walked over, looked at my work and said, "Joyce, what a wonderful page of number ones! Then she dug into her pocket, pulled out a gold star, and pasted it at the very top.

5   After running all the way home, I breathlessly entered the kitchen, shaking my paper at Mom. She exclaimed, "A gold star! I'm proud of you."

6   Disappointed, I wanted to cry, but instead I told her it wasn't about the star. "It isn't? Aren't you proud of your first gold star?"

7   "I guess. But, Mom, I made a discovery—writing!"

8   That day I discovered something grand and glorious. I found out that writing wasn't scary at all—it was exciting! I had discovered writing.

Name _____

Say Back: Listeners' Notes

Jot down your thoughts the second time the writer reads. Then, after the read, share your thoughts.

Writer 1 Name _____

I liked _____ .

I want to know more about _____ .

Writer 2 Name _____

I liked _____ .

I want to know more about _____ .

Writer 3 Name _____

I liked _____ .

I want to know more about _____ .

Writer 4: Name _____

I liked _____ .

I want to know more about _____ .

Writer 5 Name _____

I liked _____ .

I want to know more about _____ .

Name _____

Say Back: Writers' Notes

Writers, jot your notes here. You will use these notes to guide your revision.

Listeners like: _____

_____

_____

_____

_____

_____

Listeners want to hear more about: _____

_____

_____

_____

_____

Name _____

Editing Items

This paper belongs to _____

1. Is there a **name** on the paper? _____

2. Are there opening and closing **quotation marks** around **direct dialogue**?

   _____

3. Is **direct dialogue indented** for each speaker? _____

   _____

4. Is there any **indirect dialogue**? Check that it **does not** have quotation marks.

   _____

5. Are commas used correctly in any **direct addresses**? _____

   _____

6. Are there any **spelling** or **capitalization** errors? _____

   _____

7. Do the **sentences** make sense? _____

   _____

Name _____

Reflecting on My Writing

1. What did you like best about writing your personal narrative? Why?

_____

_____

2. What did you like least? Why?

_____

_____

3. What did you learn about writing? How did you learn it?

_____

_____

4. What did you learn about grammar? How did you learn it?

_____

_____

5. What did you learn about punctuation? How did you learn it?

_____

_____

6. Did you learn any new vocabulary words? What are they and how did you learn them?

_____

Name _____

Word Bank

As you listen to *Apex Predator* and think about ways to describe animals, jot down interesting words and phrases. You can use this Word Bank as a resource as you draft and revise your writing.

Name _____

Description Rubric

Use this rubric to develop and revise your draft of a description. Think about how you can improve your description to score a 4 in each category.

	Organization	Ideas & Support	Conventions
Score 4	My description introduces the animal I describe at the beginning, followed by appropriate details. I've included a strong conclusion.	My topic and reason for writing is clear. My description gives precise, descriptive details about my animal.	• My ideas are linked with words and phrases. • My writing has a variety of specific, descriptive words. • My writing has no errors in spelling, grammar, capitalization, or punctuation. There is a variety of sentence types.
Score 3	My description introduces the animal I describe near the opening. There is a conclusion.	My topic is clear, but the details are not very descriptive.	• Some of my ideas are linked with words and phrases. • Some of my words are specific. • My writing has some errors in spelling, grammar, capitalization, or punctuation. There is some variety of sentence types.
Score 2	My description gives information about the animal, but there isn't a clear opening or conclusion.	The purpose for my description is unclear or confusing. The topic is not obvious. The details are not precise or relevant.	• Ideas may be linked with words or phrases. • Few words are specific. • My writing has some errors in spelling, grammar, capitalization, or punctuation. There is little variety of sentence types.
Score 1	The introduction is not clear or is confusing about what the topic is. Details do not connect to the topic.	The topic for my description is missing and/or there are no details describing my animal.	• Ideas may not be linked with words or phrases. • No words are specific. • My writing has many errors in spelling, grammar, capitalization, or punctuation. There is no variety of sentences. Sentences are incomplete.

Name _____

My Goals

You are going to write a description about an amazing animal. A description gives details that help readers picture what is being described.

Think about your past writing. What did you do well? What do you want to do to improve your writing? Add your own goals on the lines below.

☐ Introduce the topic.

☐ Include interesting facts.

☐ Use descriptive language.

☐

☐

☐

☐

As you plan, draft, revise, and edit your description, turn back to these goals to make sure you are meeting them.

Name _____

Animal Topic List

What animal is so amazing to you that you want to research and write about it? Choose one from these lists, or write the name of a different animal.

Modern-Day Animals

☐ Siberian tiger

☐ Komodo dragon

☐ great white shark

☐ African wild dog

☐ electric eel

☐ fossa

☐ giant freshwater ray

Extinct Animals

☐ *Tyrannosaurus rex*

☐ giant short-faced bear

☐ terror bird

☐ marsupial saber-tooth

☐ *Teratorn*

☐ *Daedon*

☐ *Titanoboa*

☐ *Hatzegopteryx*

☐ *Tylosaurus*

☐ *Utahraptor*

☐ *Spinosaurus*

☐ *Mastodonsaurus*

☐ *Dimetrodon*

☐ *Dunkleosteus*

☐ sea scorpion

☐ *Trigonotarbid*

☐ *Anomalocaris*

My own choice:

_____

Name _____

Audience and Purpose

Think about who will read your description and what you want those readers to learn or understand from it. Completing this chart will help you keep your audience and purpose in mind when you begin to write.

Audience	Purpose
I will write my description for . . .	I want my readers to learn/understand . . .

Identifying Details

Complete the web by writing your topic in the center and adding the most interesting details around it.

Name _____

Description

(The Amazing Sea Pig)

1   Do you think that all pigs live on land? Well, they don't. Deep down on the ocean floor are amazing creatures called "sea pigs."

2   These animals are six-inch-long pinkish globs with pointed legs— sometimes up to seven pairs of them! They also have six whiplike growths on top of their bodies that look like antennae. And as if that weren't enough odd body parts, ten feeding tentacles surround their mouths.

3   Some scientists say their fat appearance got them the name "sea pigs," but other scientists say it's because of how they eat. Sea pigs are "deposit feeders." That means they scrounge around the deep-sea ooze for food, just like land pigs scrounge around earth mud for food. The scientific name for sea pigs is actually "scotoplanes."

4   What else is amazing about scotoplanes? They walk along the floor in the deepest, coldest, darkest part of the ocean, in search of rotting food. Hundreds of them might gather to dine on a whale carcass!

5   Scotoplanes are the only sea creatures in the group called "sea cucumbers" that have legs to walk around on. They sure don't look like cucumbers to me. Then again, they don't look like pigs either!

Name _____

Conferencing

What Catches Your Attention? Write each group member's name at the top of a column. As you listen to that writer's description a second time, take notes about what you liked or noticed: words, phrases, images, or ideas. Jot down words or phrases that will help you remember anything you wish to comment on after the reading. Use these notes when you confer with your peers about their writing.

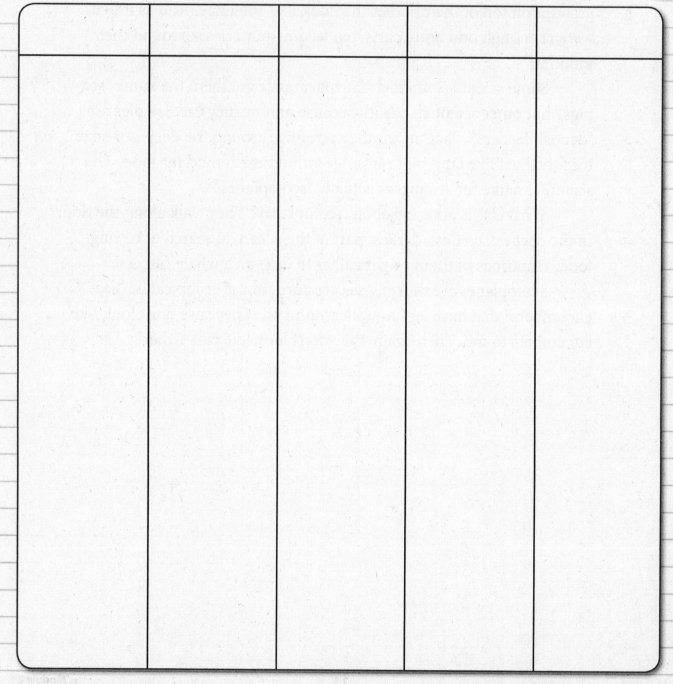

Revising

Name _____

Revision Checklist

As you revise your description, look for ways to improve your word choice by adding or combining ideas. Your revisions will help your readers more clearly picture the animal you are describing. Use this checklist to guide your revision.

☐ Did I use precise words and phrases to describe my animal?

☐ Did I use vivid verbs to describe how my animal acts or moves?

☐ Did I use sensory details?
- sight
- hearing
- taste
- smell
- touch

☐ Do adjectives and adverbs show how my animal looks and acts?

☐ Can my reader really picture my animal?

Name _____

Reflecting on My Writing

Think about the planning, writing, and publishing of your description.
Answer these questions.

What is the most amazing thing you learned about your animal?

_____

_____

_____

_____

What is one thing you learned about writing a description?

_____

_____

_____

_____

What do you like most about your description?

_____

_____

_____

_____

Name _____

Revisit My Goals

How Did I Do? Congratulations! You finished your informational description. Look at the goals you set on page 2.3. Did you meet them? What could you do better with your next piece of writing? Write two or three sentences to tell how you think you did.

_____

_____

_____

_____

_____

_____

_____

_____

_____

_____

_____

Word Bank

As you listen to *The Kite Fighters* and conduct research for your opinion essay, jot down any interesting words and phrases. You can use this Word Bank as a resource as you draft and revise your writing.

Opinion Essay Rubric

Use this rubric to develop and revise your opinion essay draft. Ask yourself if the Score 4 statements describe your writing. If not, keep revising until they do!

	Organization	Ideas & Support	Conventions
Score 4	My essay has a clear opening and a strong conclusion. Reasons are connected to the opinion with transitions.	My opinion is clearly stated in the opening of my essay, and I've included strong, relevant reasons.	• My ideas are linked with words and phrases. • My writing has a variety of specific, descriptive words. • My writing has no errors in spelling, grammar, capitalization, or punctuation. There are a variety of sentence types.
Score 3	My essay has an opening and a conclusion. Reasons may not be connected clearly to the opinion.	My opinion is in the opening of my essay but could be clearer. I've included several reasons.	• Some of my ideas are linked with words and phrases. • Some of my words are specific. • My writing has some errors in spelling, grammar, capitalization, or punctuation. There is some variety of sentence types.
Score 2	My essay may be missing an introduction or conclusion. There are no transitions connecting the reasons and opinion.	My essay's opinion is not clear. My reasons do not support my opinion.	• Ideas may be linked with words or phrases. • Few words are specific. • My writing has some errors in spelling, grammar, capitalization, or punctuation. There is little variety of sentence types.
Score 1	My essay is confusing and/or missing an introduction and conclusion.	My essay does not have a stated opinion, and/or there are no reasons for my opinion.	• Ideas may not be linked with words or phrases. • No words are specific. • My writing has many errors in spelling, grammar, capitalization, or punctuation. There is no variety of sentence types. Sentences are incomplete.

My Goals

In this module, you are going to write an opinion essay. An opinion essay expresses the writer's views on a topic.

Think about your past writing. What did you do well? What do you want to do to improve your writing? Add your own goals on the lines below.

- ☐ Clearly state my opinion.
- ☐ Provide reasons and details to support my opinion.
- ☐ Use transition words to connect ideas.
- ☐ Use persuasive language.
- ☐ Conclude with a strong restatement of my opinion.
- ☐
- ☐
- ☐
- ☐

As you plan, draft, revise, and edit your opinion essay, turn back to these goals to make sure you're meeting them.

Name _____

Brainstorming My Topic

What is my topic?

_____

_____

Time to Brainstorm! Write down as many ideas, words, and phrases about the topic that you can think of. Note every idea you have—it might spark another idea! These ideas will give you a starting point for your planning.

Name _____

Audience and Purpose

Now that you have your topic, think about who you want to read your opinion essay and your reason for writing.

Who Is My Audience?

☐ family members

☐ classmates

☐ friends

☐ general public

☐ other: _____

_____

_____

_____

What Is My Purpose for Writing?

☐ to entertain

☐ to learn

☐ to inform

☐ to persuade

☐ other: _____

_____

_____

_____

What is my opinion?

_____

_____

_____

What reasons do I have for my opinion?

_____

_____

_____

Organizing My Opinion Essay

Before you begin to draft your opinion essay, it can be helpful to put your ideas in a graphic organizer, like the one below. Write your opinion in the top box. Then add your reasons to the bottom boxes. This will help guide you as you draft.

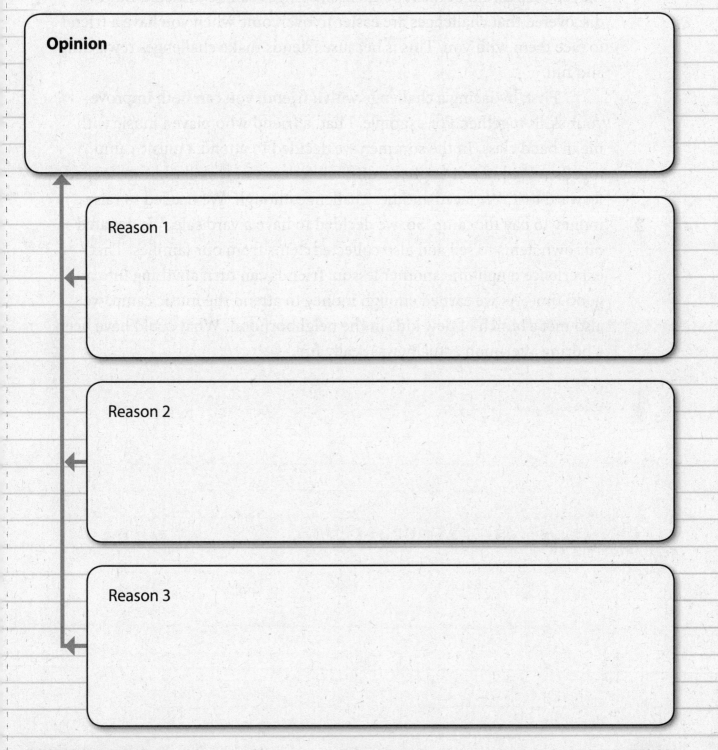

Opinion

Reason 1

Reason 2

Reason 3

Opinion Essay

Friends Make Challenges Fun

1   Do you like challenges? Many people avoid them. Sometimes, they're even afraid of them because challenges can be difficult. But I've discovered that challenges are easier to overcome when you have a friend to face them with you. This is because friends make challenges rewarding and fun.

2   First, by facing a challenge with a friend, you can both improve your skills together. For example, I had a friend who played music with me in band class. In the summer, we decided to attend a music camp together. We knew it might be difficult to learn new skills, but we looked forward to it. We faced another challenge, though. We needed to raise money to pay for camp. So, we decided to have a yard sale. We donated our own items to sell and also collected items from our families. That experience taught me another lesson: friends can turn anything into a good time. As we earned enough money to attend the music camp, we also met a bunch of new kids in the neighborhood. What could have been a boring afternoon actually was really fun.

Name _____

3   Though the idea of raising funds had seemed too difficult to us at first, my friend and I faced the challenge together. We came up with a solution, solved the problem, and were able to attend the camp. As a result, we learned some new skills, had a lot of fun together, and even made some new friends. If I had to do it alone, I'm not sure I could have. And I'm positive I wouldn't have enjoyed it nearly as much. With their laughter and conversation, friends definitely make challenges less challenging.

Name _____

Revising for Support

As you revise your writing, be sure to check that your opinion is supported by convincing reasons, facts, and examples.

Revisit the reasons you provide for your opinion statement. Ask these questions and revise any part of your essay to strengthen the support.

Questions	Original Text	Revision
Are my reasons connected to my opinion?		
Do I provide facts and examples to support my reasons?		
Are the details supporting my opinion accurate?		

As you revise, check your answer to this question.

Would I be persuaded by this support? ☐ Yes ☐ No

Name _____

Revision Checklist

An important part of the writing process is looking for ways to improve your opinion essay's sentence structure by combining and rearranging ideas for coherence and clarity. Transition words strengthen the connection between ideas. Here are some examples.

so	*although*
Everyone knew that Joni was the strongest, *so* she paddled from the front.	*Although* we lost in the final round, we held our heads high.
because	*then*
Because we worked together, we were a better team.	*Then*, we knew we had met the challenge.

Use this revision checklist to improve the sentence structure of your opinion essay.

☐ Are there sentences with related ideas that you could combine? If yes, use a comma and a coordinating conjunction to combine them.

☐ Is each idea explained fully? If not, add another sentence.

☐ Is every sentence in your draft useful and relevant to the topic? If not, delete that sentence.

☐ Do your sentences make sense in the order they appear? If not, rearrange your ideas so they do make sense.

☐ Can you make a connection between ideas stronger? If yes, use a transition word.

Name _____

Revisit My Goals

How Did I Do? Congratulations! You finished your opinion essay. Look at the goals you set on page 3.3. Did you meet them? What could you do better with your next piece of writing? Write two or three sentences that tell how you think you did.

_____

_____

_____

_____

_____

_____

_____

_____

_____

_____

_____

_____

Name _____

Word Bank

As you listen to *Love Will See You Through: Martin Luther King Jr.'s Six Guiding Beliefs*, jot down any interesting words and phrases. You can use this Word Bank as a resource as you draft and revise your writing.

Name _____

Story Rubric

Use this rubric to develop and revise your story draft. For each category, ask yourself if the statement describes your story. As you draft and revise, set a goal to score a 4 in each category.

	Organization	Ideas & Support	Conventions
Score 4	My story is told in order, and the events are clearly connected. Transitions connect the events.	My story has a clear setting, and the events are described with detail. The characters are interesting and described in detail.	• My ideas are linked with words and phrases. • My writing has a variety of specific, descriptive words. • My writing has no errors in spelling, grammar, capitalization, or punctuation. There are a variety of sentence types.
Score 3	My story is mostly told in order, and the events are mostly connected.	My story has a setting, and the events are described with little detail. The characters act and speak in a way that makes sense.	• Some of my ideas are linked with words and phrases. • Some of my words are specific. • My writing has some errors in spelling, grammar, capitalization, or punctuation. There is some variety of sentence types.
Score 2	My story has events out of order, and/or events are missing.	My story has only a part of the setting, and the events have little detail. The characters' words and actions don't make sense.	• Ideas may be linked with words or phrases. • Few words are specific. • My writing has some errors in spelling, grammar, capitalization, or punctuation. There is little variety of sentence types.
Score 1	My story is out of order, and the events are confusing.	My story does not have a setting, and/or the events are confusing. The plot is confusing.	• Ideas may not be linked with words or phrases. • No words are specific. • My writing has many errors in spelling, grammar, capitalization, or punctuation. There is no variety of sentences. Sentences are incomplete.

Name _____

My Goals

In this module, you are going to write a story. A story consists of people, places, and events.

Think about your past writing. What did you do well? What do you want to do to improve your writing? Add your own goals on the lines below.

☐ Precisely describe the person who made a difference.

☐ Include details about the events to explain how the person made a difference.

☐ Tell why I think the person's actions were important.

☐ Make sure I've spelled words correctly.

☐

☐

☐

☐

As you plan, draft, revise, and edit your story, turn back to these goals to make sure you are meeting them.

Story

The Power of Friendship

1   Last year, a new student arrived at our school. She wasn't in my grade, but my friends and I would see her around school a lot. The girl's name was Sasha, and she had moved here from another country. Sasha was having a hard time getting used to living here, so my friends and I decided to make her feel welcome. My friend Emily, in particular, went out of her way to help.

2   It wasn't long after Sasha arrived that my friends and I noticed she was having difficulty fitting in. When we were outside playing during recess, we'd notice Sasha sitting on the grass all by herself. We would be laughing, playing ball, and running around, and Sasha would just be watching us. Sometimes, she wasn't even doing that; she was just looking down. She seemed sad and lonely.

3   "What should we do?" I asked my friends.

4   Normally, Emily isn't the kind of person to just walk up to someone and start talking. She's usually really quiet and shy, especially around strangers. But she felt so bad for Sasha that she suddenly walked over and asked her, "Do you want to play?" At first, Sasha was reluctant. She just shook her head and wouldn't speak. But Emily eventually convinced her to come over. Soon, Sasha was laughing and running around with us, as if she had always been a part of our group.

Name _____

5
Not long after, we found out Sasha's birthday was coming up. Emily said, "Hey, we should throw her a surprise birthday party!" I thought this was a really nice idea because Sasha didn't know too many people she could invite to a party herself. So Emily got help from her older sister and baked Sasha a cake. Then, on Sasha's birthday, Emily made up a story about how we had to come over to her house after school. When we got to Emily's house, we surprised Sasha with the cake. She was so happy!

6
Emily took a chance by walking up to someone she didn't know and inviting her into our group. Now we all have a new friend, and Sasha is much happier. If I ever have to move to a place where I don't know anyone, I hope I meet someone like Emily.

Name _____

Planning My Story

Name the person you will write about: _____

Think About Audience and Purpose Now that you have your topic, think about who you want to read your story and your reason for writing it.

Who Is My Audience?

☐ family members

☐ classmates

☐ friends

☐ general public

☐ other: _____

What Is My Purpose for Writing?

☐ to entertain

☐ to learn

☐ to inform

☐ to persuade

☐ other: _____

What will be the conflict, or problem, in your story?

_____

_____

_____

What will be the resolution of the conflict in your story?

_____

_____

Name _____

Organizing My Story

Order Your Events Your next step is to plan the organization of your story. Use this flow chart to identify the conflict at the beginning of the story. Describe the events that follow from this conflict in the middle of the story. Then identify how the conflict is resolved at the end of the story.

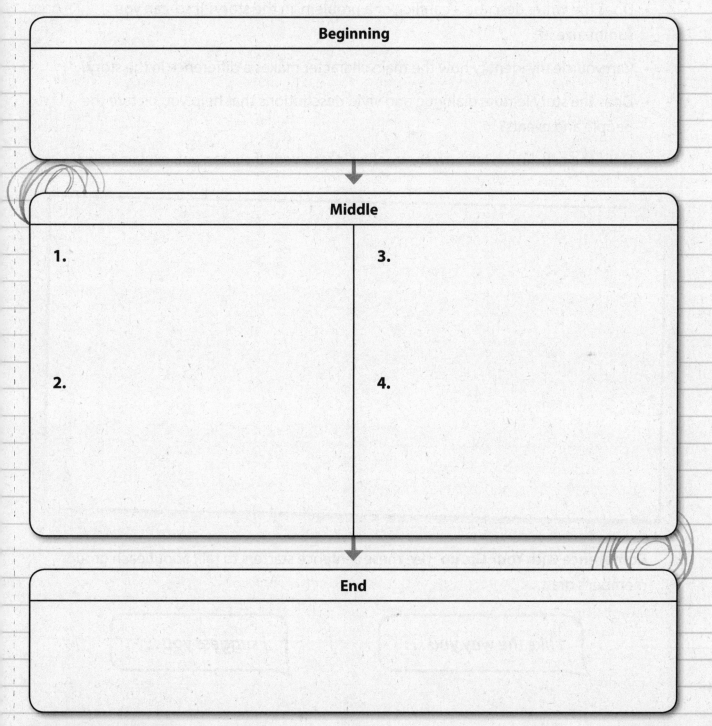

Beginning

Middle

1.

3.

2.

4.

End

Name _____

Conferencing

Highlighting Conference with your group. As you listen to each group member's story, take notes on his or her Writer's Notebook page in the space below.

- Does the writer tell where and when the story takes place?

- Does the writer describe a conflict, or a problem, in the story? If so, can you summarize it?

- Can you clearly identify how the main character makes a difference in the story?

- Does the story feature dialogue and vivid descriptions that help you picture the people and events?

- Does the conclusion tell how the conflict is resolved? If so, can you explain how?

Conference with Your Group Use these sentence starters to talk about each group member's draft.

> *I like the way you . . .*

> *I suggest you . . .*

Name _____

Revisit My Goals

How Did I Do? Congratulations! You finished your story. Look at the goals you set on page 4.3. Did you meet them? What could you do better with your next piece of writing? Write two or three sentences that tell how you think you did.

_____

_____

_____

_____

_____

_____

_____

_____

_____

_____

_____

_____

_____

_____

Name _____

Word Bank

As you listen to *Mr. Ferris and His Wheel,* write down any words and phrases that you find interesting or exciting. Listen for words that describe how Mr. Ferris and the workers who built the structure were extraordinary. You can use this Word Bank as a resource when you draft and revise your writing.

Expository Essay Rubric

Use this rubric to develop and revise your draft of an expository essay. Does each item for score 4 describe your essay? If not, keep revising until it does!

	Organization	Ideas & Support	Conventions
Score 4	My essay is organized with a clear structure. My topic is introduced in the beginning, transitions connect the ideas, and there is a strong conclusion.	My central idea is clear and focused. I use strong details, quotes, and information from my research to tell about my research topic.	• My ideas are linked with words and phrases. • My writing has a variety of specific, descriptive words. • My writing has no errors in spelling, grammar, capitalization, or punctuation. There are a variety of sentence types.
Score 3	My essay topic is clear and introduced in the beginning. I have a strong conclusion.	My central idea is clear. I include mostly relevant details. I show that I have done some research.	• Some of my ideas are linked with words and phrases. • Some of my words are specific. • My writing has some errors in spelling, grammar, capitalization, or punctuation. There is some variety of sentence types.
Score 2	My essay topic isn't clear. My conclusion isn't strong. My support isn't organized in a clear way.	My central idea isn't very well developed. My details, examples, and other information are short.	• Ideas may be linked with words and phrases. • Few words are specific. • My writing has some errors in spelling, grammar, capitalization, or punctuation. There is little variety of sentence types.
Score 1	My topic confuses my reader. There isn't a clear or strong introduction or conclusion.	My central idea isn't clear. There are few or no details, examples, or other information about my topic.	• Ideas may not be linked with words or phrases. • No words are specific. • My writing has many errors in spelling, grammar, capitalization, or punctuation. There is no variety of sentences. Sentences are incomplete.

My Goals

In this module, you will be writing an expository essay. The purpose of your expository essay is to give facts and details about an extraordinary person.

Think about your past writing. What did you do well? What do you want to do to improve your writing? Add your own goals on the lines below.

☐ Provide a clear central idea about my topic.

☐ Provide carefully researched facts and details about my topic.

☐ Use strong, interesting, and specific words to describe and explain my topic.

☐ _____

☐ _____

☐ _____

Use these goals as a checklist to develop your expository essay draft into a focused piece of writing.

Name _____

Brainstorming

Brainstorm a list of artists and other extraordinary people that you might want to write about.

_____

_____

_____

_____

Choose three people from your list that you most want to write about. Fill in the chart below. After you complete the chart, choose the person who will be the topic of your expository essay.

Topic	Pros	Cons
1.		
2.		
3.		

The topic of my expository essay is _____.

Creating a Research Plan

Complete the sentences below to create a plan for your research.

My topic is _____

_____ .

The question I want to answer in my research is _____

_____ .

Sources

- Internet sources that I might use: _____

_____

_____

- An encyclopedia entry that I might use: _____

_____

- Books that I might use: _____

_____

- Magazines that I might use: _____

_____

Take notes from your sources in your notebook or on separate paper.
Have these notes handy as you draft your expository essay.

Expository Essay

Mary Cassatt, Extraordinary Artist

1   When Mary Cassatt was just a young girl, she browsed through the art museums of Paris. She gazed at the amazing paintings. Mary knew that she wanted to become a professional artist, no matter what it took. Mary was extraordinary because of the way she courageously pursued her dream to become an artist.

2   Mary's goal was quite unusual for the 1880s in Pennsylvania. Women simply didn't become professional artists. Mary faced many hardships. Her father didn't want her to go to art school, so he did not pay for her art supplies. When she was fifteen, she went anyway, paying for her own materials. The male art students at her school in Philadelphia did not take her seriously. Finally, she moved back to Paris. There, she wasn't allowed to go to the art school, so she took private lessons. Mary studied in museums by herself.

3   Mary soon found that she didn't want to paint like the other artists. Instead, she wanted to paint women and children. Few artists did that. She wanted to try different colors. No one did that! Mary did things her way, and the paintings were wonderful!

4   After a while, other artists respected her. People liked her paintings, and they began to sell.

5   Mary Cassatt was extraordinary. She was a successful female artist who painted pictures of women and children. She changed the way other artists and the public looked at female artists.

Organizing My Essay

You have already finished the research for your expository essay. Before you begin your draft, create a flow chart. This will help you tell the events in the correct order and include all the important parts.

Title:

↓

Central Idea:

↓

Key Details:

↓

Conclusion:

Name _____

Conferencing

Listen to your classmate read his or her expository essay. Listen a second time. Then fill out the information below about the expository essay.

Writer's Name and Title of Expository Essay:

_____

_____

a. Did the writer focus on the central idea?

_____

b. Write the central idea in a single sentence.

_____

_____

c. Choose one word to express the central idea and write it here.

_____

d. Think of a synonym to express the central idea and write it here.

_____

Other notes:

_____

_____

_____

_____

_____

Name _____

Reflection

Take a few minutes to reflect on the process of writing an expository essay. Answer the following questions.

1. How did you decide which extraordinary person to use as the topic of your expository essay? Was it easy or hard to find a person to write about? Why?

    _____

    _____

2. How long did you spend doing research about this person? Why do you think it took that amount of time?

    _____

    _____

3. What was easy about writing the expository essay?

    _____

    _____

4. What was hard about writing the expository essay?

    _____

    _____

5. What advice would you give to another student who has never written an expository essay about an extraordinary person?

    _____

    _____

Name _____

Revisit My Goals

How Did I Do? Congratulations! You finished your expository essay. Look at the goals you set on page 5.3. How many of them did you meet? What could you do better with your next writing assignment? Write two or three sentences that tell how you think you did.

_____

_____

_____

_____

_____

_____

_____

_____

_____

_____

_____

Name _____

Word Bank

As you listen to *Coral Reefs* and conduct research for your formal letter, jot down any words and phrases that you find interesting or surprising. You can use this Word Bank as a resource as you draft and revise your writing.

Name _____

My Goals

In this module, you are going to write a formal letter asking for more information about a natural wonder that interests you.

Think about your past writing. What did you do well? How can you improve your writing? Add your own goals on the lines below.

- ☐ Use the correct format for my letter.
- ☐ Write a clear introduction explaining what information I would like.
- ☐ Use formal language in my letter.
- ☐
- ☐
- ☐
- ☐

Use these goals as a checklist to develop your formal letter draft into a focused piece of writing.

Formal Letter Rubric

Use this rubric to develop and revise your draft of a formal letter. Ask yourself if each statement in the rubric describes your letter. Stretch to score a 4 in each category!

	Organization	Ideas & Support	Conventions
Score 4	My letter has a properly formatted date, address, greeting, body, closing, and signature.	My topic and reason for writing is clear. My letter shows what I already know about the topic and what I hope to learn.	• My ideas are linked with words and phrases. • My writing has a variety of specific, descriptive words. • My writing has no errors in spelling, grammar, capitalization, or punctuation. There are a variety of sentence types.
Score 3	The date, address, greeting, body, closing, or signature is present but not formatted correctly.	My letter topic and/or reason for writing is confusing. I give some information about my topic.	• Some of my ideas are linked with words and phrases. • Some of my words are specific. • My writing has some errors in spelling, grammar, capitalization, or punctuation. There is some variety of sentence types.
Score 2	Part of the letter is missing, there is no request for more information.	The purpose for my letter is not clear or is confusing. The topic is not obvious.	• Ideas may be linked with words or phrases. • Few words are specific. • My writing has some errors in spelling, grammar, capitalization, or punctuation. There is little variety of sentence types.
Score 1	My letter is not formatted correctly, and/or most parts of the letter are missing.	The topic for my letter is missing, and/or I did not ask for more information about the topic.	• Ideas may not be linked with words or phrases. • No words are specific. • My writing has many errors in spelling, grammar, capitalization, or punctuation. There is no variety of sentences. Sentences are incomplete.

6.3

Name _____

Conducting Research

What is your topic?

_____

As you conduct research for your formal letter, take detailed notes to help you draft and revise your writing. Your letter must show that you already know something about the subject. Develop a research plan before beginning your research by thinking about what kinds of resources will help you.

Notes:	• It's hard to find bears to collar because the bear has to be a grizzly bear, female, and have a neck large enough so the collar won't fall off.
	• GPS collars use satellites to figure out exactly where the bear is.
	• The collars shut down from November to April, when the bears hibernate. The shutdown is to make the battery last longer.

Notes:	

6.4
Module 6

Formal Letter

As you review the model, identify the features of a letter, the request for information, and examples of formal language.

January 17, 2018
234 Green Road
Dallas, TX 75001

Mr. Everett Brown
Yellowstone National Park
PO Box 168
Yellowstone National Park, WY 82190-0168

Dear Mr. Brown:

    I recently learned that scientists use collars to track grizzly bears in Yellowstone National Park. I would love to know more about how this works. Could you please send me information about this topic or tell me where I can look to find out more about it?

    I found it interesting that the collars use a global positioning system to give the exact position of the collared bear. I also learned that the collars measure and collect data on the bear. Do you have to wait until the collar falls off to get that information?

    The work you do sounds very exciting and helpful to the bears. Thank you for taking the time to send me more information about tracking bears. I look forward to hearing from you.

Respectfully,

Alex Martinez

Alex Martinez

Name _____

Organizing My Formal Letter

Plan Your Letter Your next step is to plan the organization of your letter. Use the map to fill in necessary information and plan the body of your letter.

Date **Sender's address**		
Recipient's name and address		
Greeting followed by colon		
Body		
Introductory paragraph	Second paragraph	Closing paragraph
Closing **Handwritten signature** **Printed or typed signature**		

Conferencing

Read your partner's letter. On your partner's paper, check the box that best expresses your rating for each question.

	Great!	Really good	Just OK	Could be better	Needs help
Does the letter give you a clear idea of what kind of response the writer wants?					
Does the writer show prior knowledge of the topic?					
Do the paragraphs flow smoothly from one to another?					
Does the closing paragraph provide a satisfying conclusion?					

What is the strongest part of the letter? Why?

_____

_____

What is the weakest part of the letter? Why?

_____

_____

Name _____

Strengthening Ideas

The recipient of your letter depends on you to write coherently, or in a way that makes sense. The order of your sentences should make sense to your reader, and your ideas should be complete.

Think of it this way: if you make a friend a peanut butter and jelly sandwich, but you forget to put any peanut butter in it, your friend is going to be really confused and disappointed! Good writing makes sense, and all the ideas are complete.

As you revise your letter, improve the coherence of your writing by improving the sentence structure. Consider these tips.

☐ Are ideas missing, or does a paragraph seem incomplete? Try adding another sentence.

☐ Is every sentence important to the topic? Delete any sentences that aren't important.

☐ Do all the sentences in your letter make sense together? If not, try rearranging ideas to improve coherence.

☐ Are there sentences with the same subject or predicate? Try combining them using a comma and a conjunction.

Name _____

Revision Checklist

As you revise your letter, look for ways to improve the word choice so your reader can understand what you know about your topic and what you hope to learn.

Ask yourself these questions to help guide the revision of your letter.

☐ Are the words about your topic clear and specific? If not, use a dictionary or thesaurus to improve word choice.

☐ Does it seem like you don't introduce your topic or explain it well? If so, add some specific words or even another sentence to be clearer.

☐ Did you include a specific request for more information? Will your letter recipient understand what you want to know? If not, revise that section of your letter to clarify.

Name _____

Revisit My Goals

How Did I Do? Congratulations! You finished your letter. Look at the goals you set on page 6.2. Did you meet them? What could you do better with your next piece of writing? Write two or three sentences that tell how you think you did.

_____

_____

_____

_____

_____

_____

_____

_____

_____

_____

_____

_____

Word Bank

As you listen to *The Luck of the Loch Ness Monster*, jot down any interesting words and phrases. You can use this Word Bank as a resource as you draft and revise your writing.

Name _____

Imaginative Story Rubric

Use this rubric to develop and revise your draft of an imaginative story. For each category, ask yourself if the statement describes your story. As you draft and revise, set a goal to score a 4 in each category.

	Organization	Ideas & Support	Conventions
Score 4	My story is told in order, and the events are clearly connected. Transitions connect the events.	My story has a clear setting, and the events are described with detail. The characters are interesting and described in detail.	• My ideas are linked with words and phrases. • My writing has a variety of specific, descriptive words. • My writing has no errors in spelling, grammar, capitalization, or punctuation. There are a variety of sentence types.
Score 3	My story is mostly told in order, and the events are mostly connected.	My story has a setting, and the events are described with little detail. The characters act and speak in a way that makese sense.	• Some of my ideas are linked with words and phrases. • Some of my words are specific. • My writing has some errors in spelling, grammar, capitalization, or punctuation. There is some variety of sentence types.
Score 2	My story has events out of order, and/or events are missing.	My story has only a part of the setting, and the events have little detail. The characters' words and actions don't make sense.	• Ideas may be linked with words or phrases. • Few words are specific. • My writing has some errors in spelling, grammar, capitalization, or punctuation. There is little variety of sentence types.
Score 1	My story is out of order, and the events are confusing.	My story does not have a setting, and/or the events are confusing. The plot is confusing.	• Ideas may not be linked with words or phrases. • No words are specific. • My writing has many errors in spelling, grammar, capitalization, or punctuation. Sentences are incomplete.

Name _____

Imaginative Story

A Land Without Colors

1   A long time ago, a girl named Julia lived in a mountain village called Black-and-White Land. Everything in the village had the same three colors: black, white, or gray. The trees were black. The sky was white. The ground was gray. Everyone painted their houses one of these colors and dressed in similarly colored clothes. Julia thought the town was depressing. She hoped to move someday to a place that had other colors, like pink, blue, red, orange, green—and even brown! But for now she was stuck in Black-and-White Land.

2   One day, Julia was walking through the winding streets of her village. At the top of a steep hill, she passed by the house of an old woman. The woman was sitting at the window and motioned for Julia to come over. Julia was afraid at first. She didn't know the woman very well. She paused for a moment, not sure what to do. Eventually, she decided to at least see what the woman wanted.

3   "Can I help you?" Julia asked, as she slowly approached the woman.

4   "Young girl, I see you around the village a lot," the woman said in a creaky voice. "You never look happy. What is it that bothers you?"

5   "Well," Julia replied, "it's just that everything here is so dull. The trees are black. The sky is white. The ground is gray. There's no color anywhere." Julia dropped her head, saddened. But when she looked up again, she saw that the old woman was smiling at her.

6   "Should I tell you a secret?" the old woman asked. "I know how you can create colors whenever you want." She leaned over and whispered something in Julia's ear. Julia's eyes widened.

7   "*Really?*" she asked the old woman. The woman nodded, still smiling.

8   Julia immediately ran to the highest hill she could find, one that would give her a good view of the sky. As the old woman had instructed, Julia raised her arm and pointed her finger. Seven times, from left to right, she traced her finger in an arch across the sky. Gradually, a rainbow formed—first red, then orange, then yellow, then green, then blue, then indigo, then violet. And Black-and-White Land at long last had some color.

Name _____

My Goals

In this module, you are going to write an imaginative story. An imaginative story has interesting characters, settings, and events that may not be realistic.

Think about your past writing. What did you do well? What do you want to do to improve your writing? Add your own goals on the lines below.

☐ Include interesting characters, settings, and events.

☐ Give a creative explanation for how a natural occurrence or an animal came to exist.

☐ Use descriptive words that help the reader imagine the story.

☐ Include events in order.

☐

☐

☐

☐

As you plan, draft, revise, and edit your imaginative story, turn back to these goals to make sure you're meeting them.

Planning My Story

Which type of imaginative story will you write?

☐ fable

☐ myth

☐ tall tale

☐ legend

The *setting* is the time and place in which a story is set. What will be the setting of your story?

_____

_____

_____

Who will be the main *characters* in your story?

_____

_____

_____

What will be the main *conflict* your characters face?

_____

_____

_____

Name _____

Organizing My Imaginative Story

Order Your Events Your next step is to plan the organization of your story. Use this flow chart to tell what the story's conflict will be at the beginning of the story. Then describe the events that follow from this conflict in the middle of the story. Finally, identify how the conflict will be solved at the end of the story.

Beginning

Describe the conflict:

Middle

First event:

Second event:

Third event:

End

Describe the resolution—how the conflict is solved:

Name _____

Freewrite

Take a few minutes to freewrite about your story. Include a topic sentence at the beginning. Then provide a general overview of the story. You don't need to include a lot of details or pay close attention to your spelling or punctuation. You can include questions to yourself.

Name _____

Conferencing

Take Notes Write each group member's name at the top of a column. As you listen to that writer's story a second time, take notes about which emotions you feel at different points in the story. You can also jot down words or phrases that will help you remember anything else you liked or noticed. Use these notes when you confer with your peers about their writing.

Conference with Your Group Use these sentence frames to talk about each group member's draft.

> *When I read . . . , I felt . . .*

> *I think you did a good job . . .*

> *You might want to add . . .*

Name _____

Revisit My Goals

How Did I Do? Congratulations! You finished your imaginative story. Look at the goals you set on page 7.5. Did you meet them? What could you do better with your next piece of writing? Write two or three sentences that tell how you think you did.

_____

_____

_____

_____

_____

_____

_____

_____

_____

_____

_____

Word Bank

As you discuss and listen to *It's Disgusting and We Ate It!*, jot down any interesting words and phrases. You can use this Word Bank as a resource as you draft and revise your writing.

Name _____

Opinion Essay Rubric

Use this rubric to develop and revise your opinion essay draft. Read each item in the rubric. Strive to score a 4 in each category!

	Organization	Ideas & Support	Conventions
Score 4	My essay has a clear opening and a strong conclusion. Reasons are connected to the opinion with transitions.	My opinion is clearly stated in the opening of my essay, and I've included strong, relevant reasons.	• My ideas are linked with words and phrases. • My writing has a variety of specific, descriptive words. • My writing has no errors in spelling, grammar, capitalization, or punctuation. There are a variety of sentence types.
Score 3	My essay has an opening and a conclusion. Reasons may not be connected clearly to the opinion.	My opinion is in the opening of my essay but could be clearer. I've included several reasons.	• Some of my ideas are linked with words and phrases. • Some of my words are specific. • My writing has some errors in spelling, grammar, capitalization, or punctuation. There is some variety of sentence types.
Score 2	My essay may be missing an introduction or conclusion. There are no transitions connecting the reasons and opinion.	My essay's opinion is not clear. My reasons do not support my opinion.	• Ideas may be linked with words or phrases. • Few words are specific. • My writing has some errors in spelling, grammar, capitalization, or punctuation. There is little variety of sentence types.
Score 1	My essay is confusing and/or missing an introduction and conclusion.	My essay does not have a stated opinion, and/or there are no reasons for my opinion.	• Ideas may not be linked with words or phrases. • No words are specific. • My writing has many errors in spelling, grammar, capitalization, or punctuation. Sentences are incomplete.

Name _____

My Goals

In this module, you are going to write an opinion essay. An opinion essay gives facts and reasons in support of an idea or belief that cannot be proved.

Think about your past writing. What did you do well? What do you want to do to improve your writing? Read the following goals for writing an opinion essay. Add your own goals on the lines below.

☐ Introduce the topic.

☐ State my opinion clearly.

☐ Use strong facts to support my opinion.

☐ Include persuasive wording to convince readers to agree with my opinion.

☐ End the essay with a strong conclusion that inspires readers to take action.

☐ Use correct spelling and punctuation.

☐

☐

☐

As you plan, draft, revise, and edit your opinion essay, turn back to these goals to make sure you're meeting them.

Opinion Essay

Fishing for Good Health

1   Slimy, scaly, yuck! You don't have to travel around the world to find unusual foods. Just go to your own grocery store, and you might find a can of sardines. Peel back the lid and whole, or nearly whole, fish are lying right there inside! Sardines may not make it into most people's shopping cart, but they should. In fact, these tiny fish should be on everyone's shopping list!

2   Have you ever had a tuna sandwich? You could have almost the same sandwich made with sardines. Both types of fish are rich in protein. Sardines, though, give you more Vitamin E and more calcium than tuna. Sardines also offer heart-healthy Omega-3 fatty acids. Sardines don't have mercury in them like many larger kinds of fish, including tuna. High levels of mercury can be toxic, so sardines are a healthier choice.

3   Besides being healthful for you, sardines are also good for the environment. Sardine fisheries leave plenty of fish in the ocean, so sardines can be caught without hurting the local ecosystem. Since sardines are often canned, they have a long shelf life, limiting the amount of food waste.

4   Finally, sardines don't cost a lot of money. They are one of the cheaper foods on the shelf. When shoppers want to save money but still eat healthfully, they should grab a can of sardines.

5   Sardines are a smart choice all around, but they still aren't too popular these days. Sardines are often sold mostly intact with small, edible bones. Shoppers aren't used to buying food that looks the same as it started out. Most food these days comes chopped, mashed, fried, fileted, and otherwise changed. It might be unusual, but the benefits of sardines are too many to pass up. So, go ahead! Pull back that can lid and give sardines a try!

Name _____

Brainstorming Reasons

Think about different foods that people may not like. Consider food that your audience might find interesting or unusual. Add your ideas to the idea web.

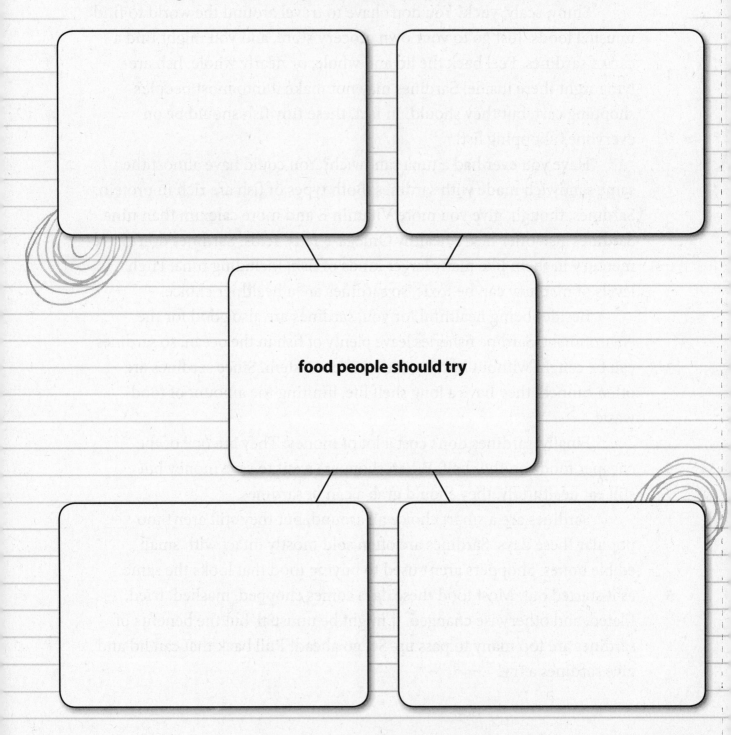

food people should try

Organizing My Essay

As you prepare to write your opinion essay, think about the reasons for your opinion. Write your reasons in the map.

Opinion:

Reason:

Reason:

Reason:

As you draft your opinion essay, turn back to these reasons to make sure you're supporting your opinion.

Conferencing

Use the following checklist as a guide during your conferences with your partner. Place a checkmark for each item that your partner's essay contains. Then describe each item from your partner's paper.

Writer's Name _____

Title of Opinion Essay _____

☐ an attention-grabbing opener

_____

_____

☐ a clearly-stated opinion

_____

_____

☐ several strong reasons that support the opinion

_____

_____

☐ transition words that show how the reasons are connected to the opinion

_____

_____

☐ a call to action

_____

_____

Reflection

1. What did you like best about writing your opinion essay? Why?

   _____

   _____

2. What did you like least? Why?

   _____

   _____

3. What was something that challenged you? What did you do?

   _____

   _____

4. Which step of the writing process was most helpful for you? Why?

   _____

   _____

5. What did you learn about writing? How did you learn it?

   _____

   _____

6. What did you learn about grammar? How did you learn it?

   _____

   _____

Name _____

Revisit My Goals

How Did I Do? Congratulations! You finished your opinion essay. Look at the goals you set on page 8.3. Did you meet them? What could you do better with your next piece of writing? Write two or three sentences that tell how you think you did.

_____

_____

_____

_____

_____

_____

_____

_____

_____

_____

_____

Name _____

Word Bank

As you listen to *The Case of the Vanishing Honeybees* and conduct research for your report, jot down any words and phrases that you find helpful, interesting, or surprising. You can use this Word Bank as a resource as you draft and revise your writing.

Name _____

Research Report Rubric

Use this rubric to develop and revise your draft of a research report. The rubric is a guide for how to improve your research report. Does each item for score 4 describe your research report? If not, keep revising until it does!

	Organization	Ideas & Support	Conventions
Score 4	My research report is organized with a clear structure. My topic is introduced in the beginning, transitions connect the ideas, and there is a strong conclusion.	My central idea is clear and focused. I use strong details, quotes, and information from my research to tell about my research topic.	• My ideas are linked with words and phrases. • My writing has a variety of specific, descriptive words. • My writing has no errors in spelling, grammar, capitalization, or punctuation. There are a variety of sentence types.
Score 3	My research topic is clear and introduced in the beginning. I have a strong conclusion.	My central idea is clear. I include mostly relevant details. I show that I have done some research.	• Some of my ideas are linked with words and phrases. • Some of my words are specific. • My writing has some errors in spelling, grammar, capitalization, or punctuation. There is some variety of sentence types.
Score 2	My research topic isn't clear. My conclusion isn't strong. My support isn't organized in a clear way.	My central idea isn't very well developed. There are not enough details and examples that support my topic.	• Ideas may be linked with words or phrases. • Few words are specific. • My writing has some errors in spelling, grammar, capitalization, or punctuation. There is little variety of sentence types.
Score 1	My topic isn't clear or is confusing. There isn't a clear or strong introduction or conclusion.	My central idea isn't clear. There are few or no details, examples, or other information about my topic.	• Ideas may not be linked with words or phrases. • No words are specific. • My writing has many errors in spelling, grammar, capitalization, or punctuation. There is no variety of sentences. Sentences are incomplete.

Name _____

My Goals

In this module, you will be writing a research report. The purpose of a research report is to provide information about a topic.

Think about your past writing. What did you do well? What do you want to do to improve your writing? Add your own goals on the lines below.

☐ Clearly state a central idea about an endangered plant or animal.

☐ Provide carefully researched facts and details.

☐

☐

☐

☐

As you plan, draft, revise, and edit your research report, return to the rubric and your list of goals to help guide your writing.

Name _____

Choosing a Topic

Choose one endangered plant or animal from these lists for your topic, or you can choose another one. Then write your research question.

Endangered Plants

South Texas ambrosia

star cactus

pecos sunflower

Texas prairie dawn

Texas snowbells

Endangered Animals

Texas horned lizard

whooping crane

Houston toad

red wolf

Kemps Ridley sea turtle

Endangered plant or animal of my choice:

_____

My research question:

_____

_____

Name _____

Creating a Research Plan

In this module, you're going to do research. Before you start your research, you need to have a plan. Answer the questions below to help you create your research plan.

1. What books or magazines will I use for my research?

   _____

   _____

2. What websites will I use for my research?

   _____

   _____

3. Do I have any personal experience that I will use in my report?

   _____

   _____

4. Is there anything else I will do for my research?

   _____

   _____

Additional Sources:

   _____

   _____

   _____

Name _____

Taking Notes

It is important to organize your notes so that you know the title and author of each source and the URL, or website address, if it comes from the Internet. If you are using a printed text, write down the page number where you found the information.

Use the cards below to take notes from your sources. List the important details. Fill out a separate card for each of your sources.

Title:
Author:
URL (if a website):
Important details:

Title:
Author:
URL (if a website):
Important details:

Name _____

Research Report

The Endangered Texas Horned Lizard

1   At 3.5 inches (8.9 cm) long, the Texas horned lizard is tiny. However, it's having big problems. The lizard is close to going extinct. If that happens, there won't be any more of the lizards. It's up to us to protect the Texas horned lizard.

2   The Texas horned lizard's scientific name is *Phrynosoma cornutum*. The name comes from the spiky spines on its head and back. The lizard's habitat is hot, dry places in the southwestern United States, especially Texas. Its gray or tan scales blend in with the sandy soil in these areas.

3   Dr. Nelson is an ecologist. She says, "The Texas horned lizard is important because it eats insect pests." So, Texas made the lizard its official state reptile. The lizard used to have a large population in Texas. But now there aren't as many of them as there used to be. People are building in its habitat. Bug sprays are killing its food.

4   The Texas horned lizard is an important part of life in Texas. It can't protect itself from what we do. It's up to us to protect it so it doesn't die out.

Name _____

Reflecting on My Writing

Take a few minutes to reflect on the process of writing a research report. Answer the following questions.

1. What did you do to come up with a research topic? Was it easy or hard to come up with a topic? Why?

   _____

   _____

2. How long did you spend doing the research? Why do you think it took that amount of time?

   _____

   _____

3. What was easy about writing the research paper?

   _____

   _____

4. What was hard about writing the research paper?

   _____

   _____

5. What tips would you give to another student who has never written a research report?

   _____

   _____

Name _____

Revisit My Goals

How Did I Do? Congratulations! You finished your research report. Look at the goals you set on page 9.3. Did you meet them? What could you do better with your next writing assignment? Write two or three sentences that tell how you think you did and what you would improve.

_____

_____

_____

_____

_____

_____

_____

_____

_____

_____

Word Bank

As you listen to *The Museum Book* and conduct research for your expository essay, jot down any interesting words and phrases. Use this Word Bank as a resource as you draft and revise your writing.

Name _____

Expository Essay Rubric

Use this rubric to develop and revise your expository essay. As you draft your essay, ask yourself if the Score 4 statements describe your writing. Revise your ideas and organization for clarity and coherence.

	Organization	Ideas & Support	Conventions
Score 4	My essay has a clear introduction and conclusion. Ideas are clearly organized in a clear structure.	My essay is focused, and the main idea is supported by facts and details.	• My ideas are linked with words and phrases. • My writing has a variety of specific, descriptive words. • My writing has no errors in spelling, grammar, capitalization, or punctuation. There are a variety of sentence types.
Score 3	My essay has an introduction and a conclusion. Most ideas are organized in a structure.	My essay is mostly focused, and the main idea is supported by some facts or details.	• Some of my ideas are linked with words and phrases. • Some of my words are specific. • My writing has some errors in spelling, grammar, capitalization, or punctuation. There is some variety of sentence types.
Score 2	My essay has an introduction or a conclusion, but one might be missing. Some ideas are organized.	My essay is not focused, and the main idea is supported by few facts or details.	• Ideas may be linked with words or phrases. • Few words are specific. • My writing has some errors in spelling, grammar, capitalization, or punctuation. There is little variety of sentence types.
Score 1	My essay is missing an introduction and a conclusion. The structure is confusing.	My essay is not focused, or the main idea is not supported by any facts or details.	• Ideas may not be linked with words or phrases. • No words are specific. • My writing has many errors in spelling, grammar, capitalization, or punctuation. There is no variety of sentences. Sentences are incomplete.

Name _____

My Goals

In this module, you are going to write an expository essay. An expository essay gives facts and details about a topic.

Think about your past writing. What did you do well? What do you want to improve in your writing? Add your own goals on the lines below.

☐ Provide a clear central idea in the introduction.

☐ Use strong, interesting verbs.

☐ Integrate research correctly.

☐ Organize with a purposeful structure.

☐

☐

☐

☐

Use these goals as a checklist to develop your expository essay draft into a focused piece of writing.

Picking a Topic

Choose a topic for your expository essay from the list below. Circle your choice.
Then, answer the questions below.

1. Greek temple	12. King Tutankhamun
2. steam locomotive	13. first plane to fly the Atlantic Ocean
3. totem pole	14. diplodocus
4. Viking ship	15. the dodo
5. diamonds	16. British Parliament buildings
6. meteorites	17. velvet ropes
7. Roman pottery	18. the bed of Queen Elizabeth I
8. Tyrannosaurus rex	19. World War I tank
9. suits of armor	20. first telephone
10. two-headed sheep	21. mummy case
11. mummy	22. first train engine

What do you already know about this topic?

_____

_____

_____

What do you want to learn about this topic?

_____

_____

_____

Name _____

Planning My Essay

What is your topic?

_____

_____

Think About Audience and Purpose Now that you have your topic, think about who you want to read your expository essay and your reason for writing.

Who is my audience?

☐ family members

☐ classmates

☐ friends

☐ general public

☐ other: _____

What is my purpose for writing?

☐ to entertain

☐ to learn

☐ to inform

☐ to persuade

☐ other: _____

Time to Brainstorm! Write down as many ideas, words, and phrases about the topic that you can think of. Note every idea you have—it might spark another idea! These ideas will give you a starting point for your research.

Conducting Research

As you conduct research for your expository essay, make sure you take good notes to help you draft and revise your writing. Make sure to include the source of the information. Put direct quotes in quotation marks.

Source:	The Museum Book by Jan Mark, page 35
Notes:	• Catherine the Great was Peter the Great's granddaughter.
	• "She was mainly interested in art."
	• "She built the State Hermitage in St. Petersburg to hold all her paintings."

Source:	
Notes:	

Source:	
Notes:	

Name _____

Organizing My Expository Essay

Plot Your Ideas Your next step is to plan the organization of your essay. Use the main idea and details map to choose your main idea and plan the order of your supporting details.

Detail:

Detail:

Main Idea:

Detail:

Detail:

Name _____

Expository Essay

The Extinct Dodo Bird

1   Imagine arriving on a tropical island, one that not many humans have ever seen. After a long voyage, it might feel great to be on land. Imagine looking around—and seeing big fluffy birds, nearly as tall as you! In the early sixteenth century, Portuguese sailors had this very experience as they laid eyes on the dodo bird. Sadly, dodo birds are extinct today, but they still fascinate people.

2   Dodo birds were native to the island of Mauritius, off the east coast of Africa. Today, we have fossil remains of dodos as well as very old stuffed birds from when they were still alive. They could be as tall as three feet and may have weighed between 23 and 40 pounds. Their feathers were likely gray and brown in color and coarse in texture. They were slow-moving and naturally curious, which caused them many problems.

3   The birds were first seen by Portuguese sailors in about 1507 ("History of the Dodo Bird"). As more European ships ventured further from the tip of Africa and into the Indian Ocean, many explorers stopped to rest and restock at Mauritius. Unfortunately for the dodo, they became an easy source of food for sailors and invasive species that traveled on the ships, such as dogs, pigs, rats, and cats. Invasive species are types of animals that are not part of a natural habitat. Dodos had no natural predators on the island, so they weren't afraid of humans and were easy prey for the invasive species.

Name _____

Conferencing

Conference with a partner. As you read your partner's expository essay, take notes on your partner's page in the space below. Use these notes to revise your draft to improve sentence structure and word choice.

- Was the central idea clearly stated?

- Did your partner make a clear promise to the reader?

- Are the specific words and phrases related to the topic?

- Does each sentence relate directly to the topic?

- Are there transition words that connect ideas to the topic?

- Did your partner use details, descriptions, facts, or examples?

- Can you remember them?

Getting Started Use these sentence starters to talk about your partner's draft.

Your topic is...

To help with ..., try ....

Name _____

Revision Checklist

An important part of the writing process is looking for ways to improve your expository essay's sentence structure and word choice.

Revisit your draft. Ask yourself these questions to help guide your revision. Remember, your expository essay should be clear and make sense to your readers.

☐ Does it seem like you don't explain an idea fully? If so, add another sentence.

☐ Is every sentence in your draft useful and relevant to the topic? If not, delete that sentence.

☐ Do your sentences make sense in the order they appear? If not, rearrange your ideas so they do make sense.

☐ Are there sentences with related ideas that you could combine? If yes, use a comma and a coordinating conjunction to combine them.

As you plan, draft, revise, and edit your expository essay, turn back to these goals to make sure you're meeting them.

Name _____

Revisit My Goals

How Did I Do? Congratulations! You finished your expository essay. Look at the goals you set on page 10.3. Did you meet them? What could you do better with your next piece of writing? Write two or three sentences that tell how you think you did.

_____

_____

_____

_____

_____

_____

_____

_____

_____

_____

_____

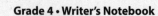

Name _____

Word Bank

As you listen to *A Strange Place to Call Home* and work through the poems, jot down words and phrases that you find interesting or surprising. You can use this Word Bank as a resource as you draft and revise your writing.

Name _____

Limerick

> There once was a boy in a tree
> Who howled when a bee stung his knee.
> The bee buzzed in return,
> So the boy said, "You'll learn!"
> And swatted the insect with glee.

Directions: Use these items to help you plan your own limerick.

Who will the poem be about? Complete the first line of the limerick below.

There once was a _____

List words that rhyme with the last word of the line (**A** rhyming words).

_____

Write a line that tells about the person and ends with an **A** rhyming word.

_____

Think of something interesting or funny that happens. Write a short line.

_____

List words that rhyme with the end word (**B** rhyming words).

_____

Write another short line that ends with a **B** rhyming word.

_____

Complete the "story." End with an **A** rhyming word. Be funny!

_____

Go back and make sure the stresses are correct in each line.

Name _____

Riddle Poem

I'm part of the daily classroom grind.
"Hey, get the lead out!" students say
As if I were slow or didn't mind.
But I make points throughout the day.
What am I?

Directions: Use these items to help you plan your own riddle poem.

Select a person, place, animal, or thing. _____

Write several words and phrases that describe the subject. Try to include
a homophone if you can.

_____

_____

Write your first line.

_____

List words that rhyme with the last word of that line (**A** rhyming words).

_____

Decide if you want to use an ABAB or AABB rhyme scheme (or something else).
As you write each line, decide which word the next line should rhyme with.
Make a group of **B** rhyming words as you need.

_____

_____

End your riddle poem with *Who* (or *What*) *am I*?

_____

Haiku and Tanka

Haiku

Monsoon rains have come.
We are soaked, dripping, soggy.
But the trees love it.

Tanka

Monsoon rains have come.
We are soaked, dripping, soggy.
But the trees love it.

Their clothes are drenched but alive
With their leaves greener than green.

Directions: Use this organizer to help you write your haiku.

1st line 5 syllables	
2nd line 7 syllables	
3rd line 5 syllables	

If your syllable count is not right, add, delete, or change words.
Now add lines in the spaces below to make a tanka.

7 syllables	
7 syllables	

Name _____

Ode

Oh weekend! How grand you are!
A break in the storm! Air to breathe!
Time to be me—to do or not do—
Free to make my own choices.

From Monday to Friday, you tempt and tease,
Like a ball of happiness bouncing just out of reach.
And then you are here, exploding with promise.
Few responsibilities! Oh the possibilities!
Too soon you must leave, but never forever.

See you next weekend!

Directions: Use this organizer to help you plan your ode.

List several topics, and then circle the one you choose for the subject of your ode.	
What do you see, hear, feel, smell, or taste, when you think about this subject?	
What action words describe this subject?	
What figurative language can you use to describe this subject?	

Now write your ode in your notebook using your plan.

Short Poems

Couplet

The trees sway in the breeze,
But their pollen makes me sneeze.

Quatrain

Humpty Dumpty sat on a wall.
Humpty Dumpty had a great fall.
All the King's horses and all the King's men
Couldn't put Humpty together again.

Tercet

The trees sway in the breeze,
But their pollen makes me sneeze.
Listen! You can hear me wheeze.

Directions: Use this organizer to help you plan your own short poems.

List several topics. Choose one for a **subject**.	
List **sensory words** about the topic.	
List **action words** about the topic.	
List **figurative language**.	
Write a line about the topic.	
List words that rhyme with the last word of that line.	
Write a second line ending with a rhyming word.	

In your notebook, write several more couplets. Next, choose a couplet and add a third line to make a tercet. Finally, combine two couplets for a quatrain, or write a quatrain with a different rhyme scheme.

Name _____

Poem Rubric

Use this rubric to develop and revise your drafts of your poems. Ask yourself if each statement in the rubric describes each of your poems. Reach to score a 4 in each category!

	Organization	Ideas & Support	Conventions
Score 4	I've used most of the different elements of poetry to express my feelings and ideas about my topic.	My poem has an engaging idea and uses sensory details, poetic techniques, and descriptive words.	• My writing has a variety of specific, descriptive words. • My writing uses punctuation and capitalization effectively. There are no errors in spelling or grammar.
Score 3	I've used some elements of poetry to express my feelings and ideas about my topic.	My poem has an idea and uses some sensory details, poetic techniques, and descriptive words.	• Some of my words are specific. • My writing uses punctuation and capitalization somewhat effectively. There are a few errors in spelling or grammar.
Score 2	I've used a few elements of poetry to express my feelings and ideas about my topic.	My poem may have an idea but uses few sensory details or poetic techniques and general words.	• Few words are specific. • My writing does not use punctuation and capitalization very effectively. There are some errors in spelling or grammar.
Score 1	I've used no elements of poetry to express my feelings and ideas about my topic.	My poem does not have an idea and does not use sensory details, poetic techniques, or descriptive words.	• No words are specific. • My writing does not use punctuation and capitalization effectively. There are many errors in spelling or grammar.

My Goals

You are going to write a series of poems in various forms on a topic that interests you.

Think about your past writing. What did you do well? How can you improve your writing? Add your own goals on the lines below.

☐ Use the correct format for my poems.

☐ Use sensory and figurative language.

☐ Challenge myself to try something new.

☐

☐

☐

☐

☐

As you plan, draft, revise, and edit your poems, turn back to these goals to make sure you are meeting them.

Name _____

Planning My Poems

Use the web to help you organize your thoughts and plan your series of poems. Write your chosen topic in the center box. In each of the other boxes, write a type of poem that you will write about the topic. Add a few notes about what features of your topic you want to focus on in each type of poem. Will your poems be separate, or will they be connected by a theme? Use the lines to jot down other planning notes.

_____

_____

_____

Name _____

Conferencing

Think about what jumps out at you as you listen to each group member read his or her poems.

What were some unusual or exciting words or words that made you think?

_____

_____

_____

What interesting similes, metaphors, or other examples of figurative language did you like?

_____

_____

_____

Which poem(s) made you laugh or really feel something about the topic? How did the writer make this happen?

_____

_____

_____

Which poem did you like the best? Why?

_____

_____

_____

Name _____

Revisit My Goals

How Did I Do? Congratulations! Well done! You finished your poems. Now look back at the goals you set on page 11.8. Did you meet them? Do you think you could have done something better or differently? What might you want to work on in your next piece of writing? Write two or three sentences that tell how you think you did.

_____

_____

_____

_____

_____

_____

_____

_____

_____

_____

Name _____

Word Bank

As you listen to *City Chickens* and conduct research for your editorial, jot down any interesting words and phrases you come across. You can use this Word Bank as a resource as you draft and revise your editorial.

Name _____

Editorial Rubric

Use this rubric to develop and revise your draft of an opinion essay. Ask yourself if the Score 4 statements describe your writing. If not, keep revising until they do!

	Organization	Ideas & Support	Conventions
Score 4	My editorial has a clear opening and a strong conclusion. Reasons are connected to the opinion with transitions.	My editorial is clearly stated in the opening of my essay, and I've included strong, relevant reasons. The call to action logically flows from my support.	• My ideas are linked with words and phrases. • My writing has a variety of specific, descriptive words. • My writing has no errors in spelling, grammar, capitalization, or punctuation. There are a variety of sentence types.
Score 3	My editorial has an opening and a conclusion. Reasons may not be connected clearly to the opinion.	My editorial is in the opening of my essay but could be clearer. I've included several reasons. There is a call to action.	• Some of my ideas are linked with words and phrases. • Some of my words are specific. • My writing has some errors in spelling, grammar, capitalization, or punctuation. There is some variety of sentence types.
Score 2	My editorial may be missing an introduction or conclusion. There are no transitions connecting the reasons and opinion.	My essay's opinion is not clear. My reasons do not support my opinion. The call to action is confusing or not clear.	• Ideas may be linked with words or phrases. • Few words are specific. • My writing has some errors in spelling, grammar, capitalization, or punctuation. There is little variety of sentence types.
Score 1	My editorial is confusing and/or missing an introduction and conclusion.	My essay does not have a stated opinion, and/or there are no reasons for my opinion. There is no call to action.	• Ideas may not be linked with words or phrases. • No words are specific. • My writing has many errors in spelling, grammar, capitalization, or punctuation. Sentences are incomplete.

Name _____

Planning

What is the topic of my editorial?

_____

_____

Think About Audience and Purpose Now that you have your topic, think about who may be reading your editorial and what they may care about. Then consider your opinion and reasons for writing the editorial. You can check more than one box in each column.

Who is my audience?	What is my purpose for writing?
☐ classmates	☐ to inform about a problem
☐ school officials	☐ to share an opinion
☐ teachers	☐ to persuade people to act
☐ parents	☐ to suggest a change
☐ other: _____	☐ other: _____

How will you get information for your editorial? Often it is necessary to do research on your topic before writing your editorial. Think about where you will get information for your editorial. Create an informal research plan, including a central research question and what sources you will consult.

My Goals

In this module, you will be writing an editorial. The purpose of most editorials is to persuade people to change their minds about an issue or to take a particular action.

Think about your past writing. What did you do well? What do you want to do to improve your writing? Add your own goals on the lines below.

☐ Clearly state an opinion about an improvement or change in my school.

☐ Think about my audience and what their opinions and concerns might be.

☐ Give specific facts and reasons to support my opinion.

☐ Use strong verbs and specific, clear word choices.

☐

☐

☐

☐

Editorial

This Is for the Birds!

1
The sounds of cheeping, chirping, and rustling wings would be a great addition to the other noises we hear every day in our schoolyard. Many beautiful birds pass through our community every spring and fall. We should install a bird feeder to help these birds as they migrate.

2
Some people might say that bird seed is expensive and that other animals would eat the seed. I talked with the owners of the local bird food shop, and they offered to donate 50 pounds of seed every year to our school. Also, the shop owners said that there are many types of bird feeders that keep other animals from getting the birds' food.

3
Our school could benefit from having a bird feeder on school property. Science classes could classify the different kinds of birds. Math classes could chart the numbers of each type of bird. Social studies classes could draw the birds' migration paths on maps and talk about the lands they fly over. Writing classes could write descriptions of the birds and their beautiful bird sounds.

4
I talked to teachers and other students, and they all think our school would be a better place if we had more feathered friends nearby. Wouldn't you like to hear cheeping, chirping, and rustling in our schoolyard, too?

Name _____

Choosing Support

Read the following sentences from an editorial. For each sentence, choose which source you think would provide the best support for the information in the sentence. Then, explain your choice.

1. Many birds migrate through our community.

☐ student surveys   ☐ bird seed package   ☐ local bird organization website

_____

_____

2. It would be easy to install and maintain a bird feeder on school grounds.

☐ school custodian   ☐ school website   ☐ school librarian

_____

_____

3. The school's parent association could give us money for a feeder.

☐ school surveys   ☐ newspaper article   ☐ association officers

_____

_____

4. Devices can keep squirrels and raccoons out of bird feeders.

☐ bird migration website   ☐ bird shop owner   ☐ science teacher

_____

_____

Name _____

Evaluating Support

Here are some sentences that could be added to the "This Is for the Birds!" editorial. For each example, circle what kind of support it is. (You may circle more than one type.) Then explain why you think the example is or is not good support.

1. The owner of the local bird feed store thinks that our school needs a bird feeder.

statistic   testimony   example   quotation   fact

Evaluation: _____

2. The teachers think a bird feeder is a good idea; 95 percent of them said so when we asked them.

statistic   testimony   example   quotation   fact

Evaluation: _____

3. Twenty years ago, many homes had bird feeders.

statistic   testimony   example   quotation   fact

Evaluation: _____

4. At a nearby school, the students enjoy having a bird feeder and seeing the variety of birds that visit there.

statistic   testimony   example   quotation   fact

Evaluation: _____

5. A magazine source says, "Bird feeders are a useful addition to school playgrounds, but their upkeep can be costly." The editorial uses these words this way: "Bird feeders . . . can be costly."

statistic   testimony   example   quotation   fact

Evaluation: _____

Name _____

Conferencing

As you read or listen to your partner's editorial, jot down answers to these questions. Use these notes to confer with your partner about the editorial.

1. Why is the first paragraph interesting? How does it preview the editorial's topic?

   _____

2. What is the writer's main point? Where is it clearly stated?_____

   _____

3. How do the paragraphs support the main idea?_____

   _____

4. Which organizational pattern did the writer use? _____

   _____

5. If the writer included an opposing idea, or straw man, how effectively did the

   writer defeat the straw man? _____

   _____

6. Does the writer need to add any facts, statistics, quotations, or other types of

   support for the main idea? If so, where? _____

   _____

7. How does the conclusion encourage readers to act? _____

   _____

8. Was the editorial convincing? Why or why not? _____

   _____

Revisit My Goals

How Did I Do? Congratulations! You finished your editorial. Look at the goals you set on page 12.4. Did you meet them? What could you do better with your next piece of writing? Write two or three sentences to tell how you think you did.

_____

_____

_____

_____

_____

_____

_____

_____

_____

_____